I0517278

Into the Milkweed Meadow

Into the Milkweed Meadow

Don Gutteridge

First Edition

Hidden Brook Press
www.HiddenBrookPress.com
writers@HiddenBrookPress.com

Copyright © 2021 Hidden Brook Press
Copyright © 2021 Don Gutteridge

All rights for poems revert to the author. All rights for book, layout and design remain with Hidden Brook Press. No part of this book may be reproduced except by a reviewer who may quote brief passages in a review. The use of any part of this publication reproduced, transmitted in any form or by any means, electronic, mechanical, photocopied, recorded or otherwise stored in a retrieval system without prior written consent of the publisher is an infringement of the copyright law.

Into the Milkweed Meadow
by Don Gutteridge

Cover Design – Sol Terlson Kennedy
Layout and Design – Richard M. Grove

Typeset in Garamond
Printed and bound in Canada
Distributed in USA by Ingram,
        in Canada by Hidden Brook Distribution

Library and Archives Canada Cataloguing in Publication

Title: Into the milkweed meadow / Don Gutteridge.
Names: Gutteridge, Don, 1937- author.
Description: Poems.
Identifiers: Canadiana 20210144742 | ISBN 9781989786314 (softcover)
Classification: LCC PS8513.U85 I58 2021 | DDC C811/.54—dc23

This collection is lovingly dedicated to
Tom, my grandson and soulmate,
who left us too soon.

Table of Contents

Twenty-One For Anne
In loving memory

Thirty-Nine For Tom
In Loving Memory

A-Burst

With a nod to e e cummings

On the just-cusp of Spring,
seedlings, breeding in the dark
under the earth, detonate,
flinging their shoots, in full
arousal, bruising upwards,
uncrumbling as they go,
rain-sated clods,
and lusting for air and a tease
of the come-summer breeze,
they sprout loudly in twos
and threes, and the world
turns as green as the groomed
desmesnes of Eden – a-burst
with birthing and bloom.

What is More

Summer was the season strung
between June and September
when we were young enough
to be free and combed
the sun-thumbed streets
for stray empties loitering
in nooks and crannies, whose
two-penny return
would buy us a grab-bag
or a brace of gumballs,
and we lazed away amber
afternoons on Canatara's
heat-seizing sands
and dove for bottle-caps
in our blue-bellied lake
and compared shy erections
in the boys' change-room
with its spy-dy hole and took
no guff from anyone
elder than us, well-meaning
or goitered, for we were easy
in our bones and, what is more,
immortal.

Undaunted

The houses of my youth haunt me
still, like the debris of my dreams
or shadows clinging to the shapes
they once made: *Mara's*
place where the roof slumped
as if too weary to sit
erect above a porch
where Gerry's Dad took
a last fall from;
Bryant's bungalow with its
manically manicured lawn
that withered when his hectic heart
exploded; *Barker's* shack
that welcomed in the Winter
wind and seething summer;
Hendries squalid colony,
each piece unpoached
by paint; *Bradley's* quaint
cottage where missus and mister
dreamed in their dotage;
the shambles of *Lumley's* shanty
in a yard where toddlers
drifted, and Grandfather's house
where I grew greening in my bardic
bones and joined in the impossible
pursuit of the perfect word:
undaunted.

True

Missus Bray, widowed
by war and still in her prime,
let her grieving flow
through the flowers that
garnished her garden, and each
bloom: crimson, gold
or blue, brought to her mind
a memory of having loved,
true and untarnished by Time.

Wordless

Missus Bradley, sunny
weather or not, stood
on her front stoop and un-
tethered a wordless cry,
heard in every nook
and cranny of the town and,
like a bee without its buzz,
wondered who she was.

Meme

Point Edward: July 2018

My village lies in quiet
collusion with the sun, long
shadows lean lengthwise
from houses that held me hostage
for a dozen seasons, and streets
my feet read like a bard's
Braille, sit just as
they did when I roamed them
like LaSalle on a sortie, combing
for news of a better world,
and the Bridge still skewers
the sky and Mara's roof
still tilts as it did
when Jerry and I swam
our summers away in the Lake
as big and as blue as the Baltic,
with dunes a-doze in the hectic
noontide light, and the school
where I scribbled the first
line of an interminable epic
is now gone under the wrecker's
ball, and I am as reluctant
to leave this meme of memory
as a bride her epithalamium
or a groom his darling's garland

Unbidden

The Widow Bray's dreams
were all of daisies and daffodils
that came unbidden in the dark
and soothed away the pain
of her bereavement, and whenever
she woke on a summer's day,
she found the sun stroking
her blooms anew and honey-
bees playing their part,
and everything that grew
hearkened to home and her heart.

Swaddled

December 1960

We stroll the Doon Pinnacle,
swaddled in the first snow.
and above us the moon looms
luminous and stars startle
the dark, and we go hand-
in-glove like pilgrims courting
a crusade, dazzled in a dimension
of delight and grateful for the gods
who dreamed us such a night
as this.

Rose

And here I am walking
the beach at Canatara
with its silken, Saharan sands
and a sun hung above,
as yellow as a bruised moon
looking for a world to enlighten
and blooming anew in the wombed
blue of the Lake I was young
enough to dream into being,
and on a far horizon, herring-
gulls levitate in loops
and cliff-swallows swerve
serenely over the dunes
I once reconnoitred
like some lunatic LaSalle,
and here is where I found
the words to ignite the poem
that grew inside me like a rose
exploding in the bone.

Agog

When the first snows come
down in a blurred fury,
children dash out into the
blizzard's bliss, let
its furred flakes tease
on the tongue, and toboggans
in tow, they seek the happiest
hill, glide gleeward
into the morning chill,
flung this way and that
in gravity's slippery grip,
and dizzy with delight at being
young enough to glow
agog at such wonders.

Balm

Christmas Eve 2020

It's easy to believe on Christmas
Eve, with snow coming down
and breathing on the sills and eaves
like a brief benediction on the
chime of silence and the chilled
dark above it, and we
are reminded of that Nazarene
scene so long ago,
when the evening sky over
Bethlehem's inn was stunned
by a star, and the Babe, calmed
by cattle lowing holy,
wakened the world to wonder,
and saint or sinner, on a night
like this, we all long
for the balm of belief.

Coiffed

Eve must have been bored
silly in the pristine desmesnes
of Eden, forever rearranging
flowers that never go a-droop
or listening to bees humming
in their hives a humdrum tune
or birds quite pleased
with their prolonged one-note
song, or counting the hours
until something other happened,
and it was forever morning
in that God-garnished garden
that never strayed into afternoon,
while helpmeet Adam wandered about,
making a fuss and wondering
what his private parts were for,
while his lady, with one eye
on an apple, just wanted
to muss his perfectly coifed
curls.

Bauble

When I was young enough
to know better, the grass
on Grandfather's lawn
had the sheen of Eden on it,
and the hedges that hugged me whole
bloomed numinous: hung
lavendered with lilacs,
and I combed those holy
grounds and the dappled shade
of the Manitoba maples,
unfettered and glowing easy
in my bones, and, like Adam,
rinsed in innocence and paradisal
light, I bedaubed whatever
I met with natural nouns
and voluptuous verbs, and all
passed peacefully in my greened
garden until, from the edge of
Everything, I heard someone
calling my name and urging me
on to the brink of Beyond,
where an apple winked like a
bright bauble on the Knowing
Tree, and I seized it with a
wordless fury.

A-Buzz

Nancy Mara, in her one-
piece suit, lies
belly-down on Canatara's
beach in its sun-seethed
sand, and for a stunned second
my breathing stalls, and my heart
purrs at the sight of wind-
thumbed thighs, and all
the boys are a-buzz, wondering
if this is what beauty was,
and something asleep
inside me leaps towards
light.

Clinch

Shirley was the first girl
no longer to be just
a pal, and I watched in awe
as she bloomed like a slow rose
in a lash of light, and when
she smiled my way, my tongue
hummed and hawed as I tried
not to ogle the fresh bevels
of her body or day-dream
a libidinous clinch,
for I knew even then
that somewhere the Earth
had moved an inch on its axis.

Lewdly

Jo-Anne, lewdly nude,
gives us full-frontal
and we zero in on her nipples
like berries dipped in sherry,
and the pink wink where
her belly goes under
and her thighs connive, and we wonder
if her desire to be desired
is deeper than the fire that fuels
our fancy, but today, it seems,
no-one wants to play
the hero of this romance,
and so, we must be content
to picture in our dreams the image
of some furious fusion.

Phalanx

When Granny Reeve died,
I remember the golden
gladioli from Mrs. Bray's
groomed garden and a casket
buried in bloom from her pied
bower, which seemed to ease
our grieving, and I thought
of Granny being carried
to Heaven on a phalanx
of flowers.

Saturdays

Saturdays were sacred
in my village, when we were freed
from the humdrum tedium
of school to make our way
to the infamous *Imperial,*
its third balcony condemned,
but who cared? it had
a Silver Screen bigger
than a boy's imagination,
with six-gun shootouts
where black-hatted villains
died bloodless for our amusement
or Gene Autry yodelled
like a Swiss miss, or the Durango
Kid, masked and mysterious,
on his alabaster mount,
or Batman and Robin, robed
and ready to put a crimp
in crime, and best of all
the cartoon, catapulted in colour
with hoodwinking Bugs
or Magoo stumbling into himself,
and these were the impudent images
that gave me a grip on story-
grammars, prompted passion
in my poetry, and enriched the thick
bailiwick of my fiction.

Friend

For Alvin Gehl in loving memory

O how I envied you,
riding your lovingly-crafted
raft like a hero in a
Mark Twain novel,
down the Mississippi
where our fantasies ended,
and me, unable to swim,
forlorn on the riverbank,
wishing I had the pluck
to play Tom to your Huck,
but you just grinned at me
as you paddled away, and said
"I'm still your friend,"

A Language for Love and Loss

I was enwombed by a village
and I strutted its pristine streets
with faetal ease, the sheen
of Eden still upon me,
giving birth to words
that sang in my genes, urgent
to be uttered, and everywhere
I glanced, the possibility
of poetry loomed, and I wrote
myself in the unreason of rhyme,
stunned literate in the celibate
sun and lanced by its light,
and I grew a language for love
and loss, and now that you
are gone where souls go
lonely to be embossed
by the universe – I have the means
of voicing a grief that burns
in me like a blister exploding
in the bone.

Derelict

In Hendrie's derelict coop
Jo-Anne does a slow-mo
strip tease, and we lick
our chops and let our eyes
graze the brazen bud
of her belly and then seize
upon the cupped crease
keeping her thighs from colliding,
and in the spirit of the day
I drop my drawers, and Jo
says, with some surprise,
"I didn't think they made them
in small sizes."

Twinned

Waterloo County, December 1960

Once again we go strolling
in taut tandem on the Doon
Pinnacle under a moon
as golden as a buccaneer's
doubloon, and starlight
wintering in the deep reaches
of the firmament and I want to
hold you aloft like a punter's
prize and soften slowly
in your blue-eyed embrace,
and we will love as if
we were twinned intimate at birth
and the world's luck was not
random

Immaculate

When I woke up in the womb,
I had no urge to leave
its amniotic ease
or brave a muscled tunnel,
but rather seemed content
to hearken to a heartbeat
and its soothing lullaby, but some-
thing deeper and more dire
thrusted me into the ambience
of an alien air, where I uttered
"I am," and all our days
since have been spent finding
a way back to that
immaculate room.

Translation

When Jo-Anne dropped her panties,
all eyes were on the prize
athwart her thighs, like a
pink wink, and we
no longer had to fantasize about
what makes a girl worth panting for
or indulge in bad-boy
banter about "broads" and "jugs,"
but something got lost
in the translation, because
whenever I gazed at a girl
thereafter, I just wanted
to hug her.

Awakening

The sun rises over
First Bush, the lava
of its light like the slow
opening of a June rose,
lacquering the leafage
and rousting robins from their
yellow-beaked sleep,
setting butterflies a-flutter
in the breath of a breeze and then
anointing a village by a Lake
with its lucid layering before
seeping agleam into alleys
and ells, and there on a
sun-strummed street
stands a boy something
like me, navigating the day's
breaking, a-dream with desire,
waiting once again
for the world's awakening.

Masculine

In a last attempt at bonding,
my father takes me hunting,
but alas I am not fond
of assassinating rabbits
or lugging a seven-pound
shotgun over field
and fallow, but the sun is summering
and my Dad's whistle sings
to something deeper inside,
and when a cottontail
erupts from the brush nearby,
my finger trembles on the trigger,
and at the sound of "Shoot! Him!"
I fire — three feet
wide, basking in the thought
I may never be masculine.

Pavillions

I craft these pieces
to ease the grip of my grief,
the ache inside that thrums
like a bone-bruise, like a
a blister in the blood, and if
I can find a soothing simile
to certify your smile
or a metaphor to instigate
your grin, the throttled throb
of my bereavement may lapse
a little like a brief breeze
dying with the afternoon
or a morning mist, lipped
adrift by the sun, or in
the pincering of a poem and the piercing
of its words, bring you back.
through the prism of my pain,
from your lonely going and into
the wide pavillions of my heart.

Ark

Noah embarked, on buffeting
seas, in an ark with a belly
full o0f beasts and their doubles,
under an oestral moon
and stars untroubled by the dark,
and when the dawn finally
erupted, a dove, dipping
its wings in the wind, sidled
to the nearest island, where
coupling creatures re-began
the world and, sure enough,
saved it for mankind.

Hectic

Missus Bray's garden
seethes with bees noshing
nectar in the petalled folds
of her flowers, and no-one
breathes an easy breath
until the last lick of light
abandons her blooms: to bide
in the arching dark, but come
morning with its ample amperage,
they rally and resume, hectic
in their pampered perfection.

Sweeter

Tim and James, rudely
nude and Rubenesque,
teeter and tumble on the
living-room rug
like fidgeting midget wrestlers
entertaining the troops,
and the winners' grin they give me,
coming up for air, tugs
something sweeter than love
and more lasting.

Chuffed

There is nothing as fabled as the coming
of Spring: poets sing
of lilacs and lilies a-flame
in the hectic heat of a May
morning and bards rhapsodize
about the redness of a rose
or daffodils buffed on a hill,
and I too have succumbed
to the pyrotechnics of June's
slow explosion in bud
and bloom, and feel a surge
of verse, vibrant in the blood,
and so chuffed I find it
in my heart to love both
Cain and Abel.

Celibate

Each summer morning
the sun boiled out of
First Bush and lashed
my village with lacquered light,
and I greeted its streets like Adam
poaching Paradise and rousted
Butch and Bones and Wiz
to reconnoitre every ell
and alley, all the way
to my boyhood beach, where,
at last, and to no-one's surprise,
I found myself alone
and celibate: with an itch for history
and a passion for poetry.

Winner

The Widow Bray grows
the best roses in town,
arching over her arbours
in loose profusion, making
their way to rose-gays
and bridal bouquets or pinned
in the curls of the girl-next-
door or her gent's linen
lapel, or tossed discreetly
in the wake of a wedding, and word
on the street: The Widow is a winner.

Blister

Adam and edible Eve
frolicked in the Garden like celibate
sisters, untingled by touch
until the Great Puppeteer
like an alcoholic embarking on a binge
or a pedophile supping on sex
furnished them with gendered flesh
and the urge to commingle, and thus
lust was born, like a blister
burnishing bone.

Demure

When Jo-Anne dropped her panties
to expose the tender tuck
where her thighs plied (I thought
of plucked roses and their dew-
wetted petals), I knew
then that girls, too,
suffered from a surfeit of lust
and the urge to lactate lips
and tantalize tongues, and O
the surge of feeling that lashed
my loins and drew me panting
into the precincts of passion,
until Jo let down her skirts
with a demure flourish, and winked.

Unblemished

For Kate

You surprised the world feet-
first, eschewing the usual
route and its womb-wrenching
penchant, and thus arrived
unblemished with eyes
as blue as agates limned
in light, and I swear you smiled
at me when they wheeled you by
and my heart burst like a
birthday balloon, and you grew
into your wee bones
like a leprechaun going for gold,
and tottered across the room into
my arms, and I will hold you so,
O my darling daughter!
until the seas run free
or the gods let my body be

Gnaw

There was Adam in God's
flawless Garden with the urge
to cleave Eve, and no
apparatus to suit, and she,
for her part, felt her heart
flutter at the sight of such
muscled might, and thus
with her id forbidden she espied
the toothsome fruit of a
nearby tree, and give it
a gnaw.

Courage

For John

You were brave before you were born,
tugged as you were down that
muscled tunnel into the world's
unwelcome, bruised and bloody
but oozing the joy of just
being you, and when I gazed
into your eyes as blue as a
heron's wind-hued
wing, my heart opened
like a morning glory lanced
by light, and you grew like a slow
oak, stalwart and straight,
at home in your bones, and I will
love you until the seas seize
or the gods give me leave
to go.

Echoes

For my grandchildren

I'll remain alive in the eyes
of my grandchildren, my genes
will breed in theirs, and I am
consoled by the notion that memories
of me, passed on through the jury
of the generations, may see
the next century and feed
on one another there,
 and when my granddaughters
arrived late in the day,
I thanked the gods who brought
such unfleeting felicity,
and now in the embering of my age
I trust the poems and stories
I plotted out of blood and bone
in a blurred fury of words,
will ferry some echoing
essence of what I was
and longed to be — to all
those who come to them
in humble expectation,
knowing that none of us
is ever wholly alone
and that language is the soul civilized.

Carolling

Christmas 2020

When we came carolling
on a Christmas Eve, snowflakes
fell as soft as a bride's
breath in her veil, and in
the dark of that numinous night
our voices sailed aloft
and it was always Hark
the Herald or Good King
Wenceslaus and we
were certain when we awoke,
easy in the wombed warmth
of our beds, that little Lord
Jesus would be sitting at our side.

Twenty-One for Anne
In loving memory

Dally

When we went walking in the wooded
wonderment below the Dune
Pinnacle, the moon hung
above, silver and serene
in a cleaved cluster of cloud,
and we talked softly with the
intimate ease of would-be
lovers, and you gave me
your hand to fold in mine
like a gift from some erotic
god, and our lips linked
in salient synchronicity
and we clung close in the
star-starved dark,
content to dally and be.

Saffron

Honeymoon Bay: July 1983

I wake from a dreamless sleep
and reach for the warm bud
of your body, but you have long
gone to your grave, and I must be
content to remember those
nights when we made love
under the aegis of the stars
and a voyeuring moon, when I thumbed
the soft sigh of your thighs
and the silken slope of your belly
with its saffron seam, and let
my fingers linger in the halo
of your hair and, unhoused
by arousal, I loved you till my blood
numbed and my bones eloped.

Joust

Once again you bedevil
my dream and we are abed,
your body bevelling mine,
your warmth a wooled welcome
as we reenact our wedding
night like lovers learning
the tacticity of touch
and the conjugal joys of our Faustian
jousting, and I want so much
to redream the long, liberating
years of our love, untouched
by the tyrannies of Time, redeemed
by two souls singing
their solos— in rhyme.

Ardent

May 1961

The first Spring to season
our affection arrived as lively
as a bride lavishing her lover
like a rosebud rupturing
ribald red, and we let it linger
simmering between us like a
gibbous moon grazing
the ardent stars, and we were
easy in our infant lusts,
knowing that love is more
than a flexing of the flesh or the lash
of allure and that Spring sometimes
comes looming in
on bashful bloom.

Muted

We whisper words of love
as if this feeling is too
fragile to be spoken above
a decibel, but still they are heard
as sweet as sunlight silking
the sill below the window
that lets the world in
to wonder at our muted
passion, and when at last
our bodies greet in full-
blooded ease, vistas
unroll, and in that cleaved
seizing, our souls are broken
and made whole again.

Doon*

December 1960

When we went walking the woods
below Doon under a sky
stitched with stars and a moon
above us, groomed luminous,
I held your hand like Galahad
cupping the Grail or a pilgrim
prizing a shrine, and I let
the light limning your eyes
linger in mine and brim
the deep December dark,
and this was a night we'll remember
long after that first
voluptuous surge of affection
has simmered, softened and lapsed
into love.

*Doon is a village in Waterloo County, Ontario

Brim

Honeymoon Bay: 1982

We pitched our tent a stone's
throw from the Bay, where wavelets
licked the shoreline
with whetted lips, and we lay
cocooned there, swaddled
in moonlight and the shadows
it shimmered, until an itch
in the innards and the soothing
collusion of our bodies brought us
upright in our bones –
unbruised on the brim
of our being.

Anodyne

On a singular summer day
I watched you swimming in Cameron,
stroking the blue-glossed
billows with an easy speed
under colluding skies,
and I thought of the morning when we woke
to find our bodies aligned
for love, and I felt such a
need to keep you afloat
forever, freed from the gossiping
gods and their petty endeavouring,
and drown in the brimming anodyne
of your eyes.

Here-And-Now

I wake from the brink of sleep
and you are in my arms
once again, as if
your death had not intervened
to lance the linkage of our lives,
and we could make love
like sweethearts in the honey
months and let our bodies,
enlinked, do their dithyrambic
dance, and I could lay
my head upon your breast
and feel your hair weeping
on my brow, and your eyes bathing me
in a blue embrace, and we
would dwell forever like moon-
struck lodgers, coupled
in the here-and-now, where nothing
dies or withers away.

Embarcation

On the night you died, the gibbous
moon refused its glow,
the stars wept a wincing
light, and Death, that passionate
assassin, bid you surrender
breath and body, like a bride
levitating her lover in the larcenous
dark, and I found you feigning
sleep on a sofa, devoid
of dream and as cold as
alabastered marble, and I cursed
the gods who fashioned such
an end to the love we bred
out of blood and ribald bone,
for I see you serene and un-
alone on a far shore
of the world, embarking for the stars.

Lustrous

I wake from a dream of you,
and you are with me once more,
alive in all your loveliness,
and we are ambling the pristine
pastures of Gibbons* as we did
when our love was young and honeyed
with hope, a daylight moon
above us like a silvered bloom,
a breeze buffeting your hair
agleam, and our hands enlinked
as if touch were tenderness
enough – and I want to drown
in the lustrous lake of your eyes
and love you unbibbed
until the world dooms or dies.

*Gibbons Park in London, Ontario

Parallels

You were always your own being,
and so our lives were doubled:
running on polished parallels,
and when the need to touch
arose, I reached into the
ozone between the rails
and felt something too
beautiful to be born aloud
and more rare than a gibbous
moon, untroubled by the dark,
and when you left me to sojourn
singular and alone, I thanked
the gods who brought you to me
and bowed to their all-seeing
hegemony.

Prudence

It was an Indian summer
afternoon when you and I
perambulated on the
Doon Pinnacle, hand-
in-glove so to speak,
your thoughts running like runes
through my head, your eyes
surprised by the gleam in mine,
and I wanted to wax iambic,
plumb the parameters of love,
stir some passion in me
unpruned by prudence.

Aloft

As I recall, it must have been
a gentling June evening
when we took our first stroll
under a moon in full
bloom in a sky un-
darkened by stars, and as
your hand softened in mine,
I felt the flutter of love,
and my heart stalled, then leapt
aloft.

Amble

Under the lactating light
of a June moon, we ambled
away our evenings, your hand
molded to mine, snug
and coveting and, above us,
where beyond begins, stars
breathed upon the dark
as if their brightening refractions
might disturb the weave
of the universe, and soon
a teasing breeze aroused
the ambient air and when,
at last, your gaze merged
with my own, I felt, then
and now, love's tug —
and somewhere where the sky dies
your soul summons and replies.

Walking, In Love

Walking, in love, under
a moon micturating light,
your hand, mellowing in mine,
stars in the beyond above,
inkling in the dark, and we
picture ourselves in the midst
of our honey months, bride
and beloved, too awkward
for talk, too adoring
to judge, content to let
our bodies abide and be,
but for the time being,
we merely embrace the evening's
breeze, easy in our pre-
nuptial nudging.

Hearken

Guelph: March 1961

It was snowing when we set out,
the weather: windless in the
chilled stillness of a March
night, flakes fluffed
in freefall, brushing branches
bridal and feathering your lashes,
your gloved hand tucked
in the pluck of mine, and I wondered
where the moon goes
in the dark far above this
whitened world, but then
all I needed is the light
abloom in your eyes to stir
in me passions that surprise,
burn in the blood and hearken
to the heart.

Heart

Strolling on a June evening
with you, gilded by moon-
glow and a million starred
particles burning through the
firmament and disbursing
intergalactic light: your hand
tucked in the pluck of mine,
we follow the shape our shadows
make, shuddering in the dubious
dark, and I am gripped
by such a feeling for lips
and eyes and the infinitesimal
flow of something that lies
between us and the heaving
heart of the universe.

Comfort

I wake and roll into the
Rubenesque bendings of your body
with all that flesh made jubilant
under the tender flensing
of a lover's touch, and even
though I'm dreaming, I am shaken
by thoughts of that silken seam
where your thighs sigh apart
and the remembrance of those nights
when we risked oblivion and rose
again, our urges purged,
and in the condoling dark
I hearken to the restless rhythm
of your breathing and the meagre
beating of your heart, and think
only that you should be here
among the living, giving me
comfort and sweetening my soul.

Thirty-Nine for Tom
In Loving Memory

Bulrushes

Into the milkweed meadow,
where puckered pods split
open to expose their silkened
seed and Monarchs nap
happily on the luff of the leaves
and butterflies bounce on the breeze
and larks tickle the air
with ardent arias and grass-
hoppers fling themselves
free of grass and gravity
and an adder weaves his way
towards Eden and bumble-
bees and their honeyed cousins
connive in their hives, and marsh
marigolds glow like van Goghs
and bulrushes, their shaggy
beards a-droop, wait
for Moses and Miriam, and I'll savour
walks like these with you
until my memory melts
or we meet in the grave.

Meander

O how I longed to take you
by the hand and meander the milk-
weed meadow abutting
Grandfather's yard,
where butterflies wobble in the
embracing breeze and puckered
pods unseam themselves
and silken in the sun, and dragonflies
dance transparent in the rarefied
air and larks levitate,
surrendering to song, and adders
gad in the grass, and I go
hob-gobling like Adam
bobbing for apples in Eden
until a poem as plump
as a petalled peony utters
itself amazing to my mind –
and I so much wanted
to have you see the seeds
of my bardic believing, but such
a luxury was not to be,
for you have gone to your grave
and I am alone with a grief
that oozes like a bruise in the bone.

Where Pain Can Breathe

My poems come from something
deep within where love abides
a-bliss in the bone and summer
is the only season when bulbs
that ruptured in the ruckus of Spring
enthuse into bloom, breeding
ballads and sonnets that seethe
with song, and I want to pin you
in the pulsing of my pentameters
and bring you back alive
and loving in the dulcet vistas
of my verse and let my grief
find a home where pain
can breathe.

Blood and Bone

In the woods above Cyprus
we follow the path paved
by bucks in pursuit of does,
and wild orchids ruffle
at our feet, lavender in pied
light, and blue jays
ruckus in the belly of a breeze
where butterflies tumble on tiny
trapezes, and a massasauga,
startled from its boggy retreat,
stutters before gliding agley,
and there is something about
a Precambrian ground older
than history and lost in its own
aloneness, and we feel the pull
of the past, the nub of being
alive here and now
and a love that binds us blood
and bone, but now you are gone
into that bleak bole,
I must be content to recall
these woodland walks
and let them ease the grist
of my grieving and sing solo
in my soul.

Serendipitous

Tom and I polling our boat
through the stream insinuating
its way between our twinned
lakes, keeping them whole
and apart, its surface honeyed
with sun, where lime-green
frogs catapult from lily-
pads and land with soft
plops among amber-hued
blooms, and a water-snake
meanders like an outcast from Eden,
and overhead a daytime
moon is hung like a bleached
doubloon, and we feel as if
our souls are summering in the ease
of this serendipitous season.

Lustrous

I wake from a dream of you,
and you are with me once more,
alive in all your loveliness,
and we are ambling the pristine
pastures of Gibbons* as we did
when our love was young and honeyed
with hope, a daylight moon
hung above us like a
bleached bloom, your hair
agleam in the buffeting breeze,
and our hands enlinked as if
touch were tenderness enough –
and I want to drown in the lustrous
lake of your eyes and love you
unbibbed until the world
dooms or dies.

*Gibbons Park in London, Ontario

Such a Night

Christmas is the season of hope,
when thoughts turn to that
mangered Babe and shepherds
shying from their sheep and Magi,
stunned by a star, strangered
in the East, follow its flight
to Bethlehem and the Holy Infant,
lalling in the stable's hay,
and cattle strummed numb
in their stalls — and centuries on,
children eased at last
into sleep, dream of reindeer
loping through the snow,
and the muffled drumbeat
of hooves upon the roof,
and Santa with his antlered escort,
full-bearded and big
of belly, and there's a magic
in the numinosity of the Nazarene's
Eve, when miracles seem oddly
ordinary, long-ago
and otherwise, and mankind
lurches towards the limned
light of love and the gift
of forgiving, and even the sting
of your untimely demise
is softened by the solace of such
a night as this.

Fugue

O Tom! I want to take you
by the hand and walk you into
the milkweed meadow a stone's
throw from Grandfather's yard,
where puckered pods secrete
their sun-drenched seed
and send their fluffed puffery
abroad, and mottled Monarchs
tilt on the brink of the breeze
or lunch on lactating leaves,
and larks decorate the day
with simmering song, and an adder
plaits the sea-grasses
with the willful weaving of his boned
belly, and down by the marsh,
marigolds marinate in a
lavishing of light and bull-
frogs bugle like a five-
piece fugue and bulrushes
shed their tufted toques —
and here, in this entranced
pasture, you and I
can soothe and savour, content
to let our souls assimilate
and be ravished random
by such beauty

Blue Blaze

I dream you once again
on Cameron's blue blaze,
and we are seated side
by side, angling for bass
grazing in the weed-seething
glades below, and you toss
your spoon in a lazy loop
and wait for the jut-jawed
bite sure-to-come,
but the afternoon softens
around us, the breeze stalls
and the lake gleams, mirroring
a new moon, silvered
in the high sky, and we are
pleased with our own company,
twinned souls in intimate
ease and a long way
from any thought that you
would soon be going where dreams
go to die and nothing blooms:
blood or bone.

Misbegotten

They say we are allotted a single
soul, but when you were born
and your blue eyes met mine
through the incubator's glass,
my soul doubled and the love
commingled with it, and you became
the hub of my happiness, blossoming
in my bones for thirty-odd
years, and I longed to keep you
safe from the jealous gods
and their unquenchable envy,
green and growing in your own
Eden, and groomed for greatness,
but now, after a brief bivouac,
you have gone where no light
looms, and I am alone
with your loss and my misbegotten
grief.

Benevolent

O Tom! I so wanted you
to grow old and benevolent
in your bones, to have your genes
seethe far into the new
century and teethe on its soothing
ertainties, and I'd like to believe
that some semblance of our being
survives long enough
to feel the heft of Heaven,
and even though you left
without a nod or goodbye,
you are alive still in the midst
of our remembering, and something
like a soul sows its seed
in my dreams and lets me gratefully
grieve your daunting odyssey.

Something of April

O Tom! My heart teems
whenever I think of you
unalive, for there was always
something of April
in the way you lunged at life,
letting it bloom in your bones
like a tulip a-burst in its bulb
or lilacs lusting after light,
or gardens seething with seed,
and there was a majesty to your mind,
its penchant for the pageantries of poetry
or the rich realms of fiction,
at home with Plato or the Bard,
a man with the several seasons
in his genes, and now that you have eased
into your preternatural sleep,
I must be content to have you
dance dithyrambs in my dreams.

In the Genes

Like lovers, we were joined at the hip,
ever since the morning
you bade farewell to the womb
with its sea-warm surround
and umbilical hug,
and your blue-eyed glance
lit up the room and the hollows
in my heart, and we rode the same
rail for thirty-five
years, hand-in-glove,
walking the woods above
Cyprus, poaching bass
on Cameron, parsing poems
in our booked nook, and when
you chose that sloe abode,
something crippled in my soul,
even as I felt the nub
of your love, teething in my genes.

A Grammar for Grief

I strolled the streets of my village
like Adam idling in Eden,
and read its ells and byways
like a blind man's fingers
breathing on Braille, and there was
poetry singing in my bones
like a meadowlark treading
air on the melodious wings
of his song, and I plumbed the rich
tillage of the home-ground
for similes and pulsing pentameters,
not knowing that one
day I would need to find
a grammar for my grief and a bardic
burst to unbenumb my blood,
still mourning your lonely
going, and longing for you
to abide, and be.

Consolation

I vaulted into my village
feet-first, and strolled its sun-
strummed streets like a
chiropodist perusing palms,
or Adam lopping fig-
leaves in the teeming green
of Eden, or a would-be bard
foraging for metaphor,
and as words surged up
in me unfettered,
I felt like a philandering prophet
singing psalms to the moon,
and so, now that you have
gone lonely to that other
home, my bereavement pain
like a boil on the bone is eased
serene in the consoling pentameters
of a poem.

A World-In-Waiting

The grass on Grandfather's lawn
was as hued as the greenery in Eden,
and when I was young and free
in my genes, I roamed its home-
ground like a sea-going
sybarite, and the hedges that hemmed
us in were hung with lilacs
like alabaster beads
stroked supple in the sun,
and shade from the Manitoba
maples dappled the dawning
dew, and I grew like a sapling
lapped by light, and never
knew there was a world-
in-waiting, where you would leave us
without the grace of goodbye
in the full fletching of your youth
for the bridal embrace of the grave,
and where loving and loss limn
us lonely, and bereavement pain
burns like a pucker in the blood
or a bruise oozing in the bone.

The Lapsing of Light

O Tom! There is no bottom
to my grief: it burns like a
throttled throb in the blood,
like a bruise burrowing
in the bone, and I so wanted you
to have an autumn to your life,
when everything alive gives a last
blast before waving goodbye:
when leaves cling to crimson
in the slow lapsing of light
and June's rose unfolds
one pink petal at a time
and apples fatten on their trees
before falling and melons
mellow around the seething
of their seed and old men
dream again of young
genes and a lonely going,
but you left us in the midst
of your living, in the soft summer
of your years, still potent
with Heaven's promise, and we
who remain must mourn your passing
and salute those days
you were good enough to give us –
in all their brutal brevity

Lyre

A note from one of your friends
tells me that you admired me,
and that news is better than a
hundred good reviews
or an invitation to dine
with the Immortals on the pastures
of Parnassus, and I knew
the moment your blue eyes
mirrored mine that love
would be our legacy, that we
would harmonize our hearts
and sing by rote a solo
so soaring it would dwarf
Orpheus and the moving music
of his lyre.

Sempiternal

Outside my window
I see the skeletal reach
of my wintering maple, and wonder
where the summer has gone
that superintended your abruption,
and whether leaves, like love,
are fated to fall away
whenever the Earth comes
autumnal, and whether with your loss
I can find the will to greet
the sprouting of a fresh, seed-
breathing Spring, embossed
with ruptured buds, knowing
you are wherever severed
souls reside, un-
interrupted by any thought
of me or the sempiternal
seizing of seasons.

Serenade

Yet another dream
of walking the woods above
Cyprus, moving through
bleached birch, feathered
fir and tufted tamarack
with sunlight beaming
the brindled umbrella aloft,
and the burr of bees, honeyed
in their hives, and wild orchids,
sheltered in the shade like shy
brides, and blue jays
enthused with their own enthusiasm,
and down by the swamp, an adder
unseams the sea-grasses,
and bloat-throated bull-
frogs belch, and we feel
the summer soaring inside
and the wide welcome of the sky
and the ghosts of those who ventured
hence to glorify their gods,
and the blood-bond we forged
on Georgian's shining shores
and, when the silence is sudden,
the serenade our souls
sing.

Basic

They say no two
souls are ever the same,
but the day my eyes first
meshed with yours in that infant's
incubator, something
more than love linked us,
bone-basic and blood-
budded, and every time
I peered into your blue
idolizing gaze, your soul
shone through and refreshed
mine.

Lazarus

If ever there be an end
to this weeping, it won't come
as long as your face floats
through the seams of my dream
or, like Lazarus, you waken
to the world once again,
or I unremember those
amber afternoons in our book-
busy nook, talking
of Tolstoy or Alfred, Lord
or the dancing of dactyls in Dylan,
as we hazarded all for love
and literature, but Death
is deeper than dying, and I must
decry the gods who ripped you
away, and weep until
the last breath betrays
my body.

Pursuit

In this dream we are once
again carousing on Cameron,
in whose blue dells
bass that might have passed
for beluga dwell in their Piscean
element, and under a cusp
of cloud herring-gulls
negotiate in eddies of air
and an osprey careens serene,
and in a far bay a lone
loon, bachelored by happenstance,
cruises through its own
reflection like a shadow over
the new moon, and the afternoon
breeze thrums like a five-
part fugue, and we are roused
by such abiding beauty
to share some part
of our common soul and pay
homage to the gods who fashioned
this place in their passionate
pursuit of perfection.

Lapse

O with what fortitude
you fought the sting of your addiction:
you entered the fray like a
paladin undaunted
on his destrier, brave and bloodied
in battle, but depression is a
bleak abode that drew you
down to its labyrinthine
darkness and tidal undertow,
and although you grinned through the
pulsing of your pain and gave us
the gist of a smile and I composed
a roseate ode to your courage,
we watched your great heart
list and give way,
sundered perhaps by the lapse
of our love.

Embrace

Into the milkweed meadow
where punctured pods release
their silkened seed and butter-
flies buffet on the breeze
and grasshoppers tease
the weeds with their athletic
leaping and larks sing
like indiffident divas and an adder
weaves in indolent ease
and bumblebees connive
in their honeycombed hive
and marsh marigolds supple
in the sun and bulrushes
ruffle scruffy in a wincing
wind, and you show no
compunction in pronouncing
this place "Paradise,"
where we can live in Nature's
bedizened embrace and where
no-one dies before their time.

Everywhere

My summer lies a-dying,
everywhere leaves unlatch,
drift like dust, hues
that bled them red and yellow
subdued, rusted, roses
in their last repose, wither,
petals thithering in the wind,
pumpkins rot in the sulking
sun, conceding their seed,
root and rhizome reach
deep, recall what
the Spring has not forgotten,
November birds, thoughts
askew, misbehave,
something in the Earth
ruptures, gives up,
and you are gone to your grave.

A-Bloom

with a nod to John B. Lee

O Tom! How I long
once again to be
with you in that room
we reserved for the meeting of our minds,
where love was never larcenous
and poems flowed as freely
as our breathing, and we talked of
iambics and righteous rhyme
and the Bard's pentameter patter
and how verse can harrow
the heart and solicit the soul,
and you had the tactful knack
of parsing my poetry and letting it
live in your eyes, and I have since
forgiven your going
and have grown oddly old
without your wise devising,
my grief: a-bloom in the bone.

Shaman

Each morning of the days
you blessed us with, you woke
in your crib and shook it like a
shaman doing St. Vitus
Dance for his elders, and later on
noontide found you
bright and bibbed with a grin
that rallied the room and a smile
that would melt a misanthrope's
gloom, and left us grateful
for the gift you gave, groomed
with love's amaze, and I wish
you had dallied a little, long
enough for me to say
my affection ran deeper
than dying or the pain of your lonely
going, that sits like a mum
budding in the bone..

Finding Felicity

Into the milkweed meadow
once more, breaking
open as we go the pouched
pods and watching their silkening
insides eddy the air,
here where grasshoppers
fling from the fringes like sassy
acrobats, and adders with bloated
throats puff umbrage,
and larks decorate the day
with song and marsh marigolds
mellow with infusions from the
celebrating sun
and cattails tuft in a buffeting
breeze: and I dream you here
with me, night upon night,
and bring you back alive
to meander meadows, find
felicity, and be.

Nook

O Tom! How I so
wanted you to grow old
in your bones, to send your genes
seething into the next century,
to whisper to your grandchildren
through the mists of memory
the name of one who first
wished you into the world
and scrawled a poem or two
you found worthy of tactful
attention, but you left without
a wave or a word of goodbye
and all the plots and thoughts
we shared, unredacted,
in our booked nook (when our love
was still green) you took
with you to the grave, and I am here
grieving what is and might have been

Dazzled

You were the love-child
we dreamed of having, born
on May Day in the morning
of the world, when all things
burst in juddering bud
and luminous bloom (like the
gleam in your eye, beguiling
a room), and we watched you grow
wholly into your bones,
stutter on a first tentative
step like a tyro on a tight-
rope, utter your fledgling
words like a poet dazzled
by the pizzazz of language and its
trilling syllables, and stand
upright and honourable
for the rest of your loving life,
and now your lonely going
has left us with our grief,
like a bruise burgeoning in the bone.

Remebering Well

I remembered you best in the misted
mornings, when the sun rose
roseate and roused the world
in an avalanche of brindled
beams, and I remembered you best
in the ambered afternoons,
when breezes breathed easily
on the maples, meandered in Grand-
father's yard, and feathered
the flowers there, and I remembered
you best in the star-brushed
evenings, when the moon mellowed
all things below
in dappled shadow and lactating
light, and now that you are gone
lonely into your grave, I must
remember you back into being,
re-alive in blood and bone
and ransacked soul, then thank
the god I don't believe in,
and carry on.

Poetry

There was so much to love
about you: your gentleness
in the way you calmed a one-
ton mare with a slow stroking
and eased its foal into the straw;
your kindness that brought you
the comfort of may friendships
and the attention of young women
y0u lavished affection on;
the majesty of your mind with the
breadth of is lexicon, the clean
seizing of ideas and the flow
of its prose; your courage in fighting
the tickle of your twin addictions:
I loved you for the light
that lilted in your eyes when you smiled
and the grin that rescued a room,
but most of all I loved you
for the poetry of your soul,
and I miss you in the first mists
of morning and in the tenuous
tilt of the dying sun, all the way
to the crack of the Doomsday
gun.

Ivy

The ivy on grandmother's wall
(for surely such a labial
leaf is feminine) climbs
the brindled, yellowing brick
in wee degrees so
infinitesimal only
the elves who share the house-
hold whenever I'm not
there can see them unlimbering
in measured millimetres
under the vimmed impetus
of the sun and the odd tickle
of rain, and sometimes at night
I think I can hear their tall
crawling towards the lip
of my room, and wish I could wake
lissomed by light – and these
are the memories, chastened by child-
hood, I longed to pass on,
but you left both them and me
to denizen some delving-
Darkness: and we must fend
for ourselves in the private precincts
of our pain.

Meadow

I am showing off the milk-
weed meadow where I spent
an afternoon of summers
among the milting greenery
and puckered pods untucking
their secret silk we waft aloft,
and where butterflies wobble
on wounded wings grass-
hoppers hop over themselves
in the wind-curried grasses
and larks in the clear air
sweeten it with song and out
on the marsh, marigolds
as orange-orbed as an autumnal
moon and cattails
with their feathered fleece,
and I am glad you're with me
to perpetuate the past
in the present, know there is a
wild child in all of us
and that love can be as deep
as the last breath before
death.

Unredeemed

I dream of those mornings
we spent cozied in the room
where books were everything,
and all our talk was of poetry
and the fevered feel of its uttered
iambic, its righteous rhyming,
the impish whim of its ironies,
of fiction enriched by the pith
of a plot, the charisma of its characters,
the lilt of its language, but literature
was never enough to keep you
alive in my eyes nor was
the way your wit lit up
my life, and though my grief
goes unredeemed by time,
there is little left in this world
when loving dies.

Don Gutteridge was born in Sarnia and raised in the nearby village of Point Edward. He taught High School English for seven years, later becoming a Professor in the Faculty of Education at Western University, where he is now Professor Emeritus. He is the author of more than seventy books: poetry, fiction and scholarly works in educational theory and practice. He has published twenty-two novels, including the twelve-volume Marc Edwards mystery series, and forty books of poetry, one of which, *Coppermine*, was short-listed for the 1973 Governor-General's Award. In 1970 he won the UWO President's Medal for the best periodical poem of that year, "Death at Quebec." To listen to interviews with the author, go to: http://there-andthen.podbean.com. Don lives in London, Ontario.

www.ingramcontent.com/pod-product-compliance
Lightning Source LLC
Chambersburg PA
CBHW030916140626
46545CB00017B/2484